I ♥ MY

|||||||||||||||||||||||||||||||||||||||||||||||||||||||||||||||||||||||||||||||||||||

WAFFLE MAKER

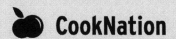 CookNation

I LOVE MY WAFFLE MAKER
THE ONLY WAFFLE MAKER
RECIPE BOOK YOU'LL EVER NEED

ISBN 978-1-911219-94-1

DISCLAIMER

CONTENTS

WHOLE WHEAT WAFFLES & HEALTHIER TOPPINGS 49

BAKED-IN FLAVOUR WAFFLES 61

HOMEMADE SYRUPS & FRUIT COMPOTES 75

OTHER COOKNATION TITLES 86

INTRODUCTION

So you love waffles! Who doesn't?

From sweet to savoury, deliciously decadent to healthier whole wheat: waffles are the ultimate comfort food. Quick, easy & satisfying they hit the spot every time with very little mess OR washing up.

Whether you are treating yourself or making a family feast, waffles are perfect for any meal. With the toppings of your choice they're superb for breakfast, lunch, dinner or any snack in between.

Contained in this recipe collection you'll find waffle ideas for all tastes and occasions. Whether simple sweet waffles with sumptuous syrups or healthier whole wheat savoury waffles you'll find something here to love.

This is a general recipe book to suit all waffle makers. You'll need to tailor the quantities to suit your own device size and always ensure you follow your manufacturers instructions and operations manual - as it may differ in cooking methods and timings to the directions included in this collection.

A key thing to remember is not to overfill your waffle maker regardless of the suggested serving quantities in the recipes.

IF YOU HAVEN'T ALREADY BOUGHT YOUR WAFFLE MAKER HERE ARE A FEW THINGS TO CONSIDER BEFORE MAKING A PURCHASE

- Try to choose a model which provides consistent, even heat. You want your waffles to turn out crispy and golden brown every time.

- A preheating light is essential – that way you'll know when you can pour in your waffle batter.

- It's great if your device has a timer so you know when your waffles are ready.

- Non-stick heating grids are a must (all modern models should have these as standard). You need the waffles to be easily removable from the grids after cooking and a non-stick surface facilitates this.

- Ideally you are looking for a device which has removable grids, this makes the cleaning process so much easier.

HINTS & TIPS

- Always pre-heat your Waffle Maker before using.

- Keep the lid of the Waffle Maker closed whilst pre-heating.

- For even waffles pour the batter onto the centre of each grid and spread out evenly to the edges.

- Do not over fill the grids with batter.

- Waffles are best served hot, straight after cooking.

- If you are making a big batch of waffles you can keep the cooked waffles warm in a pre-heated oven (do not wrap in foil or anything else as they will get soggy).

- Allow waffle mixture to rest for at least five minutes before using.

- Always unplug the machine before cleaning.

- Ensure you clean your waffle maker carefully after each use.

- Make sure you read your appliance manual carefully with regard to safety, operation, cleaning & maintenance.

ABOUT COOKNATION

CookNation is the leading publisher of innovative and practical recipe books for the modern cook.

With a range of #1 best-selling titles - from the innovative 'Skinny' calorie-counted series, to the 5:2 Diet Recipes collection and I Love My range - CookNation recipe books have something for everyone.

Visit **www.bellmackenzie.com** to browse the full catalogue.

SWEET WAFFLES & TOPPINGS

SIMPLE SWEET WAFFLE MIX

Makes 8-10 waffles

INGREDIENTS

- 300g/11oz plain/all purpose flour
- 2 tbsp sugar
- 1 tbsp baking powder
- ½ tsp baking soda
- Pinch of salt
- 380ml/1½ cups skimmed milk
- 90ml/⅓ cup vegetable oil
- 2 eggs

METHOD

1 Add all the ingredients to a large bowl and mix well until you have a smooth batter.

2 Allow the batter to rest for at least 5 minutes and preheat your Waffle Maker.

3 When the waffle maker is fully heated pour approximately 90ml/⅓ cup of batter into the centre of each grid. Take care not to overfill the grids.

4 Close the lid and allow to cook for approx. 5 minutes or until the waffles are cooked through and piping hot.

5 When the waffles are ready open the lid, carefully remove from the waffle maker and serve whilst still warm.

CHEFS NOTE

These basic waffles are great with just a dusting of icing sugar and a drizzle of maple syrup.

APRICOT BRANDY BUTTER TOPPING

Makes topping for 1 person

INGREDIENTS

- 75g/3oz dried apricots
- 120ml/½ cup brandy
- 1 tbsp brown sugar
- 50g/2oz unsalted butter

METHOD

1 Finely chop the dried apricots and add to a saucepan with the brandy.

2 Place over a medium heat and bring to the boil.

3 Reduce the heat and simmer for a few minutes or until most of the brandy has reduced.

4 Remove from the heat and stir through the butter and sugar.

5 Place back over a gentle heat and stir until the sugar dissolves.

6 Tip the apricot butter on top of the waffles and serve.

CHEFS NOTE

You don't have to use alcohol for this recipe, you could just soak the apricots in warm water to rehydrate, drain and then add to the pan with the butter and sugar.

HOT FUDGE TOPPING

INGREDIENTS

- 125g/4oz milk chocolate
- 50g/2oz butter
- 250ml/1 cup sweetened Condensed Milk
- 2 large scoops vanilla ice cream

METHOD

1 Finely chop the chocolate.

2 Add the butter to a saucepan and melt over a gentle heat.

3 Add the chopped chocolate and stir until melted.

4 Add the condensed milk in and continue stirring until the butter is fully combined and the chocolate has melted.

5 Place the ice cream on top of the waffles, drizzle the fudge sauce all over the top and serve.

CHEFS NOTE

This is a really simple fudge sauce using only 3 ingredients.

WHISKEY WHIPPED CREAM TOPPING

INGREDIENTS

- 250ml/1 cup whipping cream
- 1 tbsp whiskey
- 1 tbsp icing sugar

METHOD

1 Add the cream and whiskey to a bowl and whisk to combine.

2 Add the icing sugar and continue to whisk until the cream stiffens up a little.

3 Place the cream on top of the waffles and serve.

CHEFS NOTE

Double cream or whipping cream is fine for this recipe. Adjust the icing sugar to suit your own taste.

CARAMELIZED BANANA TOPPING

Makes topping for 1 person

INGREDIENTS

- 1 banana
- 50g/2oz butter
- 1 tbsp brown sugar

METHOD

1 Peel & slice the banana.

2 Add the butter to a saucepan and melt over a gentle heat.

3 Add the sugar and stir until the sugar is fully dissolved.

4 Add the sliced banana and gently cook until the banana caramelizes.

5 Pour the bananas and syrup over the top of the waffle and serve.

CHEFS NOTE

The banana is caramelized when it turns a gentle golden colour.

CLASSIC BANANA SPLIT TOPPING

Makes topping for 1 person

INGREDIENTS

- 1 banana
- 1 cherry
- 1 tbsp peanuts
- 2 tbsp whipped cream
- 1 large scoop vanilla ice cream
- 2 tsp chocolate chips
- 1 tbsp chocolate sauce

METHOD

1 Peel the banana and split in half lengthways.

2 Cut the cherry in half and finely chop the peanuts.

3 Assemble the banana split by laying the banana halves on top of the waffle.

4 Add the ice cream, cream and cherry halves

5 Drizzle the chocolate sauce on top.

6 Sprinkle with chocolate chips and nuts to serve.

CHEFS NOTE

Banana split is a classic waffle topping which is tough to improve on.

EASY APPLE CRUMBLE TOPPING

Makes topping for 2 people

INGREDIENTS

- 2 apples
- 1 tbsp brown sugar
- 1 tbsp water
- 4 digestive biscuits

METHOD

1 Peel, core and dice the apples

2 Add the apples, brown sugar and water to a saucepan and bring to the boil. Reduce the heat and leave to gently stew for 5-8 minutes or until tender.

3 Whilst the apples are stewing place the digestive biscuits into a plastic bag. Bash the bag with a rolling pin until the biscuits turn into crumbs.

4 When the apples are ready tip on top of the waffles.

5 Sprinkle the biscuit crumbs all over and serve.

CHEFS NOTE

Super fast crumble: great with cream or custard too.

MAPLE CREAM TOPPING

INGREDIENTS

- 2 tbsp soft cheese
- 2 tsp icing sugar
- 1 tbsp maple syrup
- 4 fresh walnuts
- ½ tsp ground cinnamon

METHOD

1 Beat together the soft cheese and icing sugar.

2 Add the maple syrup and combine well.

3 Halve and chop the walnuts.

4 Spread the soft cheese over the top of the waffle and top with chopped walnuts.

5 Dust with the ground cinnamon to serve.

CHEFS NOTE

A soft cheese such as Philadelphia is ideal for this topping.

SWEET PECAN TOPPING

Makes topping for 1 person

INGREDIENTS

- 2 tbsp pecans
- 50g/2oz unsalted butter
- 1 tbsp brown sugar
- 60ml/¼ cup maple syrup

METHOD

1 Finely chop the dried pecans.

2 Add the butter to a saucepan and gently heat to melt.

3 Add the sugar and combine until the sugar is dissolved.

4 Stir through the maple syrup and chopped pecans until warmed.

5 Tip the sweet pecans over the top of the waffle and serve.

CHEFS NOTE

You could use any type of nuts you prefer for this topping and feel free to add some ice cream too!

'TIRAMASU' WAFFLE TOPPING

Makes topping for 1 person

INGREDIENTS

- 125g /4oz mascarpone cheese
- 1 tbsp condensed milk
- ½ tsp vanilla extract
- 1 tbsp coffee liqueur
- 1 tsp cocoa powder

METHOD

1 Beat together the mascarpone, milk and vanilla extract until smooth.

2 Add the liqueur and combine.

3 Top the waffle with the mascarpone mixture.

4 Sift the cocoa over the top and serve.

CHEFS NOTE

The waffle takes the place of the traditional sponge fingers in this unconventional twist on tiramisu.

SWEET & SALTY TOPPING

Makes topping for 1 person

INGREDIENTS

- 2 slices pancetta
- Olive oil
- 2 tbsp maple syrup
- 1 scoop vanilla ice cream

METHOD

1 Finely chop the pancetta.

2 Gently sauté the pancetta in a saucepan, with a tiny drizzle of olive oil, for a few minutes until crisp and golden.

3 Add the maple syrup, remove from the heat and stir though to warm.

4 Tip the pancetta and warm syrup over the waffle.

5 Sit the ice cream on top and serve.

CHEFS NOTE

Sweet syrup and salty pancetta make this a lovely more-ish topping. Feel free to use any type of bacon you have.

CARAMEL BUTTERCREAM TOPPING

INGREDIENTS

- 50g/2oz butter
- 50g/2oz icing sugar
- 50g/2oz caramel sauce

METHOD

1 Let the butter warm to room temperature.

2 Cut the softened butter into small cubes and place in a bowl.

3 Sift the icing sugar over the butter to get rid of any lumps and beat through until creamy and combined.

4 Add the caramel sauce and beat well to create a consistent mixture.

5 Place in the fridge for 5 minutes to firm up before serving on top of your warm waffle.

CHEFS NOTE

This is a decadent topping best saved for lazy weekends.

AMERICAN PUMPKIN CREAM TOPPING

Makes topping for 1 person

INGREDIENTS

- 50g/2oz butter
- ½ tsp ground cinnamon
- 2 tbsp tinned pumpkin puree
- 1 tbsp honey
- ½ tsp vanilla extract

METHOD

1 Let the butter warm to room temperature

2 Cut the softened butter into small cubes & place in a bowl with the cinnamon and pumpkin puree.

3 Beat until light and fluffy.

4 Add the honey and vanilla and continue to beat for 2 minutes until smooth.

5 Place in the fridge for 5 minutes to firm up before serving on top of your warm waffle.

CHEFS NOTE

Tinned pumpkin puree is widely available in both the UK & US.

BUTTERSCOTCH & WALNUT TOPPING

INGREDIENTS

- 100g/3½oz caster sugar
- 3 tbsp warm water
- 25g/1oz butter
- 300ml/11floz double cream
- Handful of fresh walnuts

METHOD

1 Gently dissolve the caster sugar with the water in a small saucepan over a low heat.

2 Increase the heat and bring to the boil for a moment but do not stir it.

3 When the sugar turns dark whisk in the butter.

4 Remove from the heat and stir in double cream.

5 Chop the walnuts and sprinkle over the waffles.

6 Tip the butterscotch sauce over the top and serve.

CHEFS NOTE

This topping works equally well with pecan nuts.

STRAWBERRY WAFFLE PUDDING

Makes pudding for 2 people

INGREDIENTS

- 4 sweet waffles
- 2 tsp melted butter
- 150g/5oz strawberries, chopped
- 75g/3oz milk chocolate chips
- 250ml/1 cup crème fraiche
- 50g/2oz caster sugar
- 2 tsp plain flour
- ½ tsp vanilla extract
- 2 eggs, beaten
- 1 tbsp icing sugar

METHOD

1 Preheat the oven to 200C/400F/Gas 6.

2 Brush a baking dish with the melted butter.

3 Break the waffles into bite-sized pieces and place in the dish.

4 Sprinkle over the chopped strawberries & chocolate and combine well.

5 In a separate bowl mix together the caster sugar, flour, crème fraiche and vanilla extract, then whisk in the eggs.

6 Pour this over the waffles in the baking dish and bake in the oven for 20-25 minutes or until cooked through and piping hot.

7 Dust with icing sugar and serve.

CHEFS NOTE

This delicious oozy waffle pudding is great served with vanilla ice-cream.

CHOCOLATE CUSTARD TOPPING

INGREDIENTS

- 250ml/1 cup single cream
- ½ tsp vanilla essence
- 3 egg yolks
- 1 tbsp sugar
- 50g/2oz milk chocolate chips

METHOD

1 Combine the cream and vanilla essence in a small saucepan over a gentle heat and bring to a simmer.

2 Remove from the heat and leave to cool for 5 minutes.

3 Beat together the egg yolks and sugar and slowly whisk this into the cream in the pan.

4 Place the pan back on a gentle heat and warm through until the custard thickens.

5 Add the chocolate chips and stir until melted.

6 Serve warm over hot waffles.

CHEFS NOTE

Homemade custard can be tricky. Make sure you keep everything at a low temperature to prevent curdling.

SAVOURY WAFFLES & TOPPINGS

BASIC SAVOURY WAFFLES

INGREDIENTS

- 250g/9oz plain/all purpose flour
- 1 tbsp sugar
- 1 tbsp baking powder
- 430ml/1¾ cups milk
- 100g/3½oz melted butter
- 3 eggs

METHOD

1 Add the flour, sugar & baking powder to a large bowl and mix well.

2 In a separate bowl beat together the milk, melted butter and eggs & stir this into the flour mixture until you have a smooth batter.

3 Allow the batter to rest for at least 5 minutes and preheat your Waffle Maker.

4 When the waffle maker is fully heated pour approximately 90ml/⅓ cup of batter into the centre of each grid. Take care not to overfill the grids.

5 Close the lid and allow to cook for approx. 5 minutes or until the waffles are cooked through and piping hot

6 When the waffles are ready open the lid, carefully remove from the waffle maker and serve whilst still warm.

CHEFS NOTE

Add a teaspoon of salt to the batter if using unsalted butter.

FRESH SALSA, EGG & CHIVE TOPPING

INGREDIENTS

- 1 large ripe tomato
- ¼ red onion
- Pinch dried chillies
- 1 tbsp freshly chopped coriander
- 1 tsp lime juice
- ½ tsp sea salt
- 1 large egg
- 1 tsp oil
- 1 tbsp chopped chives

METHOD

1 Finely dice the tomato and onion.

2 In a bowl combine the chopped tomatoes, onion, dried chilies, coriander, lime juice and salt to make a simple salsa.

3 Add the oil to a frying pan over a medium setting and heat for a minute or two.

4 Crack the egg into the pan, cover and cook for 3-4 minutes or until the white is solid and the yolk is still slightly runny.

5 Pile the egg and salsa on top of your savoury waffle, sprinkle with chopped chives and serve.

CHEFS NOTE

Adjust the balance of lime and chilli in the salsa to suit your own taste.

MANGO & AVOCADO TOPPING

Makes topping for 1 person

INGREDIENTS

- ¼ ripe mango, peeled & stoned
- ½ ripe avocado, peeled & stoned
- 2 spring onions
- 2 tsp lime juice
- Pinch of red chilli flakes
- Pinch of salt
- 1 egg
- 1 tsp oil

METHOD

1 Dice the mango and avocado. Finely chop the spring onions.

2 In a bowl gently mix together all the ingredients, except the egg & oil, and set to one side once combined.

3 Add the oil to a frying pan over a medium setting and heat for a minute or two.

4 Crack the egg into the pan, cover and cook for 3-4 minutes or until the white is solid and the yolk is still slightly runny.

5 Sit the fried egg on your waffle and pile the mango mixture on top.

CHEFS NOTE

Mango and avocado are a classic combination packed with good fats and energy

MEXICAN SWEET POTATO TOPPING

Makes topping for 1 person

INGREDIENTS

- 1 sweet potato, diced
- 2 tsp olive oil
- 1 tsp chilli powder
- 1 tsp cumin
- 1 tsp turmeric
- Pinch salt & pepper
- 1 tbsp sour cream
- 2 spring onions, diced
- 4 cherry tomatoes, diced
- 25g/1oz feta cheese

METHOD

1 Preheat the oven to 400F/200C/Gas 6

2 Combine the cubed sweet potato, oil, dried spices, salt & pepper in a bowl.

3 Spread the oily potatoes out on to a nonstick baking sheet and cook for 15-20 minutes or until tender, turning once during cooking.

4 When the potatoes are ready. Dollop the sour cream on top of the waffle and tip over the sweet potatoes over along with the chopped tomatoes and spring onions.

5 Crumble the feta cheese over the top and serve.

CHEFS NOTE

Feel free to add some fresh chopped chillies and coriander to garnish.

BEEF CHILLI & CHEESE TOPPING

Makes topping for 4-6 people

INGREDIENTS

- ½ onion, chopped
- 1 celery stick, chopped
- 1 garlic clove, crushed
- 1 tsp olive oil
- 500g/1lb 2oz lean minced beef
- 2 tsp chilli powder
- 1 tsp dried oregano
- 200g/7oz tinned kidney beans
- 400g/14oz tinned chopped tomatoes
- 1 tbsp tomato puree/paste
- ½ tsp salt
- 200g/7oz grated cheddar cheese

METHOD

1 Gently sauté the onion, celery and garlic in a saucepan with a little oil for a few minutes until softened and golden.

2 Add the beef and stir-fry until the meat is browned.

3 Add the chilli powder, oregano, kidney beans, chopped tomatoes, puree & salt. Combine well, cover and leave to simmer for about 20 minutes on a low heat, stirring occasionally.

4 Check the beef is cooked through and piping hot (cook for a little longer if there is too much liquid).

5 Pile the chilli on top of the waffles and sprinkle with cheese.

CHEFS NOTE

Store any leftovers in the fridge or freezer.

CREAMY MUSHROOM TOPPING

Makes topping for 1 person

INGREDIENTS

- 2 shallots
- 1 garlic clove
- 150g/5oz mushrooms, sliced
- 60ml/¼ cup cream
- 2 tsp olive oil
- 1 tbsp freshly chopped flat-leaf parsley
- Salt and freshly ground pepper

METHOD

1 Slice the shallots & mushrooms. Crush the garlic clove.

2 Gently sauté the shallots, garlic and mushrooms in a saucepan with a little oil until softened and tender.

3 Add the cream and cook for a few minutes longer until everything is warmed through and creamy.

4 Pile the mushrooms on top of the waffles and sprinkle with the chopped parsley.

5 Season with the salt and pepper and serve.

CHEFS NOTE

If you have any to hand add a little dried thyme to the mushrooms whilst they are sautéing.

HOLLANDAISE & BACON TOPPING

Makes topping for 2 people

INGREDIENTS

- 4 slices back bacon
- 6 tbsp white wine vinegar
- 9 peppercorns
- 1 dried bay leaf
- 4 egg yolks
- 250g/9oz melted butter
- Dash of lemon juice
- Salt and pepper to taste

METHOD

1 Preheat the grill to a medium heat and cook the bacon slices until crispy.

2 Meanwhile add the vinegar, peppercorns and bay leaf to a small saucepan over a high heat. Let the vinegar bubble until it reduces to about a third of its original volume.

3 Remove from the heat and strain away the peppercorns & bay leaf.

4 Put the egg yolks in a food processor along with the strained vinegar.

5 Turn on the food processor whilst slowly pouring in the melted butter. The sauce will start to thicken. If it gets a little too thick add a splash of hot water and pulse again.

6 Season with salt and pepper and a dash of lemon juice.

7 Pour the sauce over the waffles and top with the crispy bacon slices.

CHEFS NOTE

Hollandaise sauce can be a bit tricky, but it's delicious when you get it right.

PROSCIUTTO & PARMESAN TOPPING

Makes topping for 1 person

INGREDIENTS

- 2 large eggs
- 2 tsp butter
- 2 slices prosciutto
- Salt & pepper to taste
- 1 tbsp Parmesan shavings

METHOD

1 Beat the eggs in a bowl with the salt & pepper.

2 Melt the butter is a saucepan on a medium heat.

3 Pour the eggs into the melted butter and stir for a minute or two until the eggs begin to scramble.

4 Remove from the heat and tip the eggs onto the waffles.

5 Top with the prosciutto, Parmesan shavings and plenty of black pepper.

CHEFS NOTE

When scrambling the eggs take them off the heat a moment before they are ready. They will continue to cook in their own residual heat and should be just perfect as you serve.

SMOKED SALMON & AVOCADO TOPPING

Makes topping for 1 person

INGREDIENTS

- ½ ripe avocado, peeled & stoned
- ¼ red onion,
- 2 slices smoked salmon
- Lemon wedge
- 1 tsp extra virgin olive oil
- Salt & black pepper to taste

METHOD

1 Cut the avocado half into 4 slices.

2 Finely slice the red onion in half moons.

3 Place the smoked salmon slices on the waffle and squeeze a little of the lemon on the salmon.

4 Arrange the onion and avocado slices on top of the salmon and drizzle with olive oil.

5 Add some seasoning and serve with the lemon wedge on the side.

CHEFS NOTE

A tablespoon of cream cheese dolloped on the side makes a nice addition to this lovely topping.

FRESH FIG & RICOTTA TOPPING

INGREDIENTS

- 2 figs
- 2 tbsp ricotta cheese
- 2 tsp extra virgin olive oil
- Salt & black pepper to taste
- 2 tsp honey

METHOD

1 Cut the figs into 4 slices.

2 Gently combine the ricotta cheese and olive oil together with some seasoning.

3 Place the cheese on the waffle. Top with the sliced figs and drizzle the honey over the top.

CHEFS NOTE

Although this is a savoury topping a little honey makes a lovely accompaniment to the ricotta cheese.

SPINACH & GRUYERE CHEESE TOPPING

INGREDIENTS

- ½ onion
- 1 tsp olive oil
- 2 handfuls fresh spinach leaves
- 50g/2oz grated gruyere cheese
- Salt & pepper to serve

METHOD

1 Peel and chop the onion.

2 Remove any thick stalks from the spinach leaves.

3 Gently sauté the onion in a saucepan with the olive oil for a few minutes until softened and golden.

4 Add the spinach to the pan and wilt for a minute.

5 Place the spinach and onions on top of the waffles and sprinkle the cheese over the top.

6 Season with salt & pepper to serve.

CHEFS NOTE

You could also add a little mild mustard to the spinach whilst it is wilting.

RED PEPPER & FETA TOPPING

INGREDIENTS

- 1 red pepper
- 2 spring onions
- 2 tsp olive oil
- 1 tsp freshly chopped mint
- 50g/2oz feta cheese
- Salt & pepper to serve

METHOD

1 Deseed and slice the pepper. Chop the spring onions.

2 Gently sauté the pepper and spring onions in a saucepan with the olive oil for a few minutes until softened and golden.

3 Add the mint, stir through and remove from the heat.

4 Place the peppers and onions on top of the waffles and crumble the feta cheese over the top.

5 Season with salt & pepper to serve.

CHEFS NOTE

You could also add some diced avocado to this simple waffle topping.

SQUASH & STILTON TOPPING

Makes topping for 1 person

INGREDIENTS

- 200g/7oz butternut squash
- 2 tsp olive oil
- 60ml/¼ cup vegetable stock
- Handful of rocket
- 50g/2oz Stilton cheese
- Salt & pepper to serve

METHOD

1 Deseed, peel and finely dice the squash.

2 Gently sauté the squash in a saucepan with the olive oil for a few minutes until golden.

3 Add the stock, cover and simmer for 8-10 minutes or until the squash is tender and cooked through.

4 Drain any stock from the pan. Add the rocket & Stilton, quickly stir through to combine everything and remove from the heat.

5 Pile everything on top of the waffles.

6 Season with salt & pepper and serve.

CHEFS NOTE

If you prefer the Stilton melted leave the pan on the heat for a minute or two longer.

BUTTERY SAVOY & BACON TOPPING

Makes topping for 1 person

INGREDIENTS

- 2 slices back bacon
- ¼-½ head savoy cabbage
- 1 tbsp butter
- 25g/2oz grated cheddar cheese
- Salt & pepper to serve

METHOD

1 Preheat the grill to a medium heat and cook the bacon slices until crispy.

2 Shred the savoy cabbage into bite-sized pieces.

3 Gently melt the butter in a saucepan and sauté the cabbage for a few minutes until softened.

4 Chop the crispy bacon and add to the pan along with the grated cheese.

5 Combine everything for a minute or two and remove from the heat.

6 Pile everything on top of the waffles. Season with salt & pepper and serve.

CHEFS NOTE

You can use any type of cabbage you prefer for this recipe. Add as much butter as you like and serve with lots of black pepper.

QUICK SPICED RAITA TOPPING

INGREDIENTS

- ¼ cucumber
- 2 tbsp Greek yoghurt
- 1 tsp ground cumin
- 1 garlic clove, crushed
- 1 tsp lemon juice
- Pinch of dried crushed chillies
- Salt & pepper to season

METHOD

1 Peel and dice the cucumber.

2 In a bowl gently mix together all the ingredients until combined.

3 Pile everything on top of the waffle.

4 Season & serve.

CHEFS NOTE

Add a pinch of dried chillies to serve if you wish along with a little freshly chopped mint.

WEDDING BREAKFAST

INGREDIENTS

- 1 egg
- 50g/2oz spinach
- 2 tsp butter
- 1 tbsp creme fraiche
- 1 tbsp chives
- 2 slices smoked salmon
- Salt & pepper to serve

METHOD

1 Bring a pan of water to a hard simmer and gently poach the egg for a couple of minutes.

2 Meanwhile gently heat the butter in a saucepan and wilt the spinach.

3 Combine the creme fraiche with the chopped chives and season with salt and pepper.

4 Top the waffles with the wilted spinach followed by the smoked salmon slices.

5 Dollop the crème fraiche on the top and season with lots of black pepper.

CHEFS NOTE

This topping will make any day special. No need to save it for your wedding day!

BLT

INGREDIENTS

- 2 slices back bacon
- 2 vine ripened tomatoes
- ¼ iceberg lettuce
- 1 tbsp mayonnaise
- Salt & pepper to taste

METHOD

1 Preheat the grill to a medium heat and cook the bacon slices until crispy.

2 Meanwhile slice the tomatoes and shred the lettuce.

3 Assemble your BLT by laying the bacon over the top of the waffle.

4 Top with shredded lettuce and sliced tomatoes

5 Add a dollop of mayo to the side to serve.

CHEFS NOTE

Fresh and filling. This sandwich combo works just as well as a waffle topping.

BACON & FRIED BANANA TOPPING

Makes topping for 1 person

INGREDIENTS

- 1 banana
- 2 slices streaky bacon
- 1 ripe tomato
- 1 tsp olive oil
- 1 tbsp butter
- Salt and freshly ground pepper

METHOD

1 Please and cut the banana into 2cm/1 inch slices.

2 Quarter the tomato.

3 Gently cook the bacon and tomato in a saucepan with a little oil for a few minutes. When the bacon is brown and the tomatoes are soft put to one side.

4 Add the butter to the pan and begin frying the banana slices on a medium to high heat. Cook for 1-2 minutes each side.

5 Pile the bacon, tomatoes and fried bananas on top of the waffles and serve.

CHEFS NOTE

A seemingly peculiar combination that is strangely satisfying.

PARMESAN GARLIC 'BREAD'

INGREDIENTS

- 50g/2oz butter
- 1 tbsp flat leaf parsley
- 1 garlic clove
- 1 tsp grated Parmesan cheese

METHOD

1 Take the butter out of the fridge to bring to room temperature.

2 Finely chop the parsley.

3 Crush the garlic clove.

4 Combine the softened butter together with the parsley, garlic and cheese until completely combined.

5 Spread the butter over the top of the waffle & serve.

CHEFS NOTE

This is a waffle twist on garlic bread. Delicious.

HUMMUS GREEK TOPPING

INGREDIENTS

- ½ ripe avocado
- 2 sundried tomatoes
- 3 black olives
- 1 tbsp hummus
- 2 tsp balsamic vinegar
- Drizzle of olive oil

METHOD

1 De-stone the avocado half and slice into a fan shape.

2 Finely chop the sundried tomatoes.

3 Pit and finely chop the olives.

4 Combine the chopped olives and tomatoes with the hummus.

5 Spread the hummus over the waffle.

6 Sit the avocado on top and drizzle with olive oil & balsamic vinegar to serve.

CHEFS NOTE

Another beautiful savoury waffle this time inspired by Greek flavours.

RATATOUILLE TOPPING

INGREDIENTS

- 2 aubergines
- 4 courgettes
- 2 yellow peppers
- 5 tbsp olive oil
- 2 garlic cloves, crushed
- 1 onion, sliced
- 2 tbsp chopped basil
- 200g/7oz tinned chopped tomatoes
- 1 tbsp red wine vinegar
- 1 tsp sugar

METHOD

1 Chop the aubergine and courgettes into bite sized chunks.

2 Deseed and slice the peppers.

3 Add the oil to a large saucepan and gently sauté the aubergine, courgettes, peppers, onion and garlic for a few minutes until softened.

4 Add the red wine vinegar and cook for a minute or two longer.

5 Stir through the sugar and chopped tomatoes.

6 Season well and leave to gently simmer for 10-15 minutes or until everything is softened, cooked through and well combined.

7 Sprinkle with basil and serve with savoury waffles.

CHEFS NOTE

Use whichever vegetables you have to hand for this simple ratatouille.

WHOLE WHEAT WAFFLES & HEALTHIER TOPPINGS

BASIC WHOLE WHEAT WAFFLES

Makes 8-10 waffles

INGREDIENTS

- 125g/4oz whole-wheat flour
- 125g/4oz plain/all purpose flour
- 2 tsp brown sugar
- 1 tbsp baking powder
- 1 tsp salt
- 2 eggs
- 340ml/1⅓ cups milk
- 75g/3oz melted butter
- 1 tsp vanilla extract

METHOD

1 Add the whole-wheat flour, plain flour, sugar, baking powder & salt to a large bowl and mix well.

2 In a separate bowl beat together the eggs, milk, melted butter and vanilla extract then stir this into the flour mixture until you have a smooth batter.

3 Allow the batter to rest for at least 5 minutes and preheat your Waffle Maker.

4 When the waffle maker is fully heated pour approximately 90ml/⅓ cup of batter into the centre of each grid. Take care not to overfill the grids.

5 Close the lid and allow to cook for approx. 5 minutes or until the waffles are cooked through and piping hot

6 When the waffles are ready open the lid, carefully remove from the waffle maker and serve whilst still warm.

CHEFS NOTE

A great base to experiment with your favourite 'healthy' toppings.

CHERRY & CRÈME FRAICHE TOPPING

Makes topping for 1 person

INGREDIENTS

- 1 tbsp low fat crème fraiche
- 1 tsp agave nectar
- 2 tbsp frozen black cherries
- 2 tbsp frozen mango

METHOD

1 Take the frozen fruit out of the freezer and leave to defrost- you can do this overnight in the refrigerator.

2 Gently combine the thawed fruit together with the crème fraiche.

3 Pile the creamy fruit on top of your whole wheat waffle, drizzle the agave nectar over the top and serve.

CHEFS NOTE

You could use fat free Greek yogurt on place of the creme fraiche.

MIXED BLITZED BERRY TOPPING

INGREDIENTS

- 2 tbsp blueberries
- 1 tbsp raspberries
- 4 strawberries
- 1 tsp agave nectar
- 1 tsp water

METHOD

1 Hull and slice the strawberries.

2 Add all the fruit to a blender and pulse for a few seconds.

3 Add all the ingredients to a saucepan and gently warm on the stove for a few minutes.

4 Taste the fruit and adjust the agave nectar to suit your on taste.

5 When it's warmed through remove from the heat and allow to cool for a minute or two to thicken up.

6 Pour over your whole-wheat waffle and serve.

CHEFS NOTE

You could use any mix of berries you wish for this or a different sweetener if you prefer.

ALMOND PEACHES & ICE CREAM

INGREDIENTS

- 3 peach slices, tinned
- 1 tbsp low fat vanilla ice cream
- 1 tsp fresh almonds

METHOD

1 Take the ice cream out of the freezer to thaw slightly.

2 Drain and dice the peach slices.

3 Mash the ice cream a little with the back of a fork to soften and then combine with the diced peach.

4 Pile the ice cream over the whole wheat waffle.

5 Sprinkle with chopped almonds and serve.

CHEFS NOTE

Almonds are a good source of protein, fibre and are naturally low in sugar.

GOAT'S CHEESE & SPINACH TOPPING

Makes topping for 1 person

INGREDIENTS

- 1 tbsp low fat goat's cheese
- 50g/2oz baby spinach
- 1 tsp water
- Salt & black pepper

METHOD

1 Rinse the spinach and remove any thick stalks.

2 Add the spinach to a saucepan and gently wilt on the stove for a minute with the water.

3 Add the goat's cheese and combine over a gentle heat.

4 When it's warmed through remove from the heat and pile on top of the whole-wheat waffle.

5 Season with salt and lots of black pepper to serve.

CHEFS NOTE

Goat's cheese is a good source of calcium, protein & vitamin A.

ALMOND BUTTER & FRUIT TOPPING

Makes topping for 1 person

INGREDIENTS

- ½ banana
- ½ apple
- 1 tbsp almond butter
- Pinch ground cinnamon

METHOD

1 Peel and slice the banana.

2 Peel, core and chop the apple.

3 Spread the almond butter over the top of the waffle.

4 Pile the chopped fruit on top of your whole-wheat waffle.

5 Sprinkle a pinch of cinnamon over the top to serve.

CHEFS NOTE

Low fat peanut butter makes a good substitute for almond butter.

HERBY COTTAGE CHEESE TOPPING

Makes topping for 1 person

INGREDIENTS

- ½ lemon
- 1 tsp chives
- 1 tsp flat leaf parsley
- 2 tbsp cottage cheese
- Salt & black pepper

METHOD

1 Zest the lemon and put to one side.

2 Finely chop the chives and parsley and combine these together the cottage cheese.

3 Pile the cottage cheese on top of the whole wheat waffle

4 Sprinkle the lemon zest over the top.

5 Season with salt and plenty of black pepper to serve.

CHEFS NOTE

Cottage cheese is a good low fat/high protein topping.

GRATED FRUIT & MINT TOPPING

INGREDIENTS

- ½ apple
- ½ pear
- 1 melon slice
- 1-2 tsp low fat Greek yoghurt
- Bunch of mint leaves

METHOD

1 Peel & core the apple and pear.

2 Use a grater to gently grate the apple, pear and melon slice.

3 Finely chop the mint.

4 Combine the grated fruit with just enough of the yoghurt to hold it together

5 Pile the fruit on top of the whole wheat waffle.

6 Sprinkle with chopped mint and serve.

CHEFS NOTE

This is a super, low fat topping. Use whichever fruit you have to hand.

CACAO NIBS & BANANA TOPPING

Makes topping for 1 person

INGREDIENTS

- 1 banana
- 1 tbsp cacao nibs
- 1 tbsp pecans

METHOD

1 Peel and mash the banana with the back of a fork.

2 Finely chop the pecans.

3 Pile the mashed banana on top of the whole-wheat waffle.

4 Sprinkle the cacao nibs & pecans over the top and serve.

CHEFS NOTE

Cacao nibs are the least processed and most natural form of chocolate. They are a wonderful source of fibre and magnesium.

ROASTED TOMATO TOPPING

INGREDIENTS

- 2 handfuls of cherry tomatoes
- Handful of rocket
- 2 tsp olive oil
- 2 tsp balsamic vinegar
- Salt & black pepper

METHOD

1 Preheat the oven to 400F/200C/Gas Mark 6

2 Cut the tomatoes into halves. Place in a bowl and combine with the oil, salt & pepper.

3 Lay the tomatoes out onto a baking tray and cook in the oven for 10-15 minutes or until the tomatoes are soft and cooked through.

4 Remove from the oven, place the tomatoes into a bowl and gently combine with the balsamic vinegar and rocket.

5 Tip the tomatoes on top of the whole wheat waffle and serve.

CHEFS NOTE

Use sweet ripe cherry tomatoes for this savoury topping.

BAKED-IN FLAVOUR WAFFLES

BANANA BROWN SUGAR WAFFLES

Makes 8-10 waffles

INGREDIENTS

- 300g/11oz plain/all purpose flour
- 2 tbsp brown sugar
- 2 tsp baking powder
- 1 tsp baking soda
- ½ tsp salt
- 2 eggs
- 90ml⅓ cup vegetable oil
- 200g/7oz Greek yoghurt
- 180ml/¾ cup milk
- 2 ripe bananas

METHOD

1 Add the flour, sugar, baking powder, baking soda & salt to a large bowl and mix well.

2 In a cup beat together the eggs and oil and add to the flour bowl along with the yoghurt and milk. Stir until you have a smooth batter.

3 Peel and mash the bananas with the back of a fork. Fold this into the batter until combined.

4 Allow the batter to rest for at least 5 minutes and preheat your Waffle Maker.

5 When the waffle maker is fully heated pour approximately 90ml/⅓ cup of batter into the centre of each grid. Take care not to overfill the grids.

6 Close the lid and allow to cook for approx. 5 minutes or until the waffles are cooked through and piping hot.

7 When the waffles are ready open the lid, carefully remove from the waffle maker and serve whilst still warm.

CHEFS NOTE

Sprinkle a little extra sugar over the top of these before serving if you wish.

LUXURY CHOCOLATE WALNUT WAFFLES

Makes 8-10 waffles

INGREDIENTS

- 175g/6oz plain/all purpose flour
- 100g/3½oz sugar
- 2 tbsp cocoa powder
- 1½ tsp baking powder
- ½ tsp baking soda
- Pinch of salt
- ½ tsp cinnamon
- 250ml/1 cup milk
- 1 egg, beaten
- 1 tsp vanilla extract
- 75g/3oz melted butter
- 2 tbsp chocolate chips
- 2 tbsp chopped walnuts

CHEFS NOTE

Perfect served with whipped cream and chocolate sauce.

METHOD

1 Add the flour, sugar, cocoa powder, baking powder, baking soda, salt and cinnamon to a large bowl & mix well.

2 Add the milk, egg and vanilla extract & stir well until you have a smooth batter. Add the melted butter & chocolate chips and mix until combined.

3 Allow the batter to rest for at least 5 minutes and preheat your Waffle Maker.

4 When the waffle maker is fully heated pour approximately 90ml/⅓ cup of batter into the centre of each grid. Take care not to overfill the grids.

5 Close the lid and allow to cook for approx. 5 minutes or until the waffles are cooked through and piping hot

6 When the waffles are ready open the lid, carefully remove from the waffle maker and serve whilst still warm sprinkled with chopped walnuts.

DUSTED CINNAMON WAFFLES

Makes 8-10 waffles

INGREDIENTS

- 300g/11oz plain/all purpose flour
- 1 tbsp brown sugar
- 2 tbsp baking powder
- ½ tsp baking soda
- 2 tsp ground cinnamon
- ½ tsp salt
- 380ml/1½ cups skimmed milk
- 90ml/⅓ cup vegetable oil
- 2 eggs, beaten
- 1 tbsp icing sugar

METHOD

1 Add all the ingredients, except the icing sugar, to a large bowl and mix well until you have a smooth batter.

2 Allow the batter to rest for at least 5 minutes and preheat your Waffle Maker.

3 When the waffle maker is fully heated pour approximately 90ml/⅓ cup of batter into the centre of each grid. Take care not to overfill the grids.

4 Close the lid and allow to cook for approx. 5 minutes or until the waffles are cooked through and piping hot

5 When the waffles are ready open the lid, carefully remove from the waffle maker, dust with icing sugar and serve whilst still warm.

CHEFS NOTE

Tap the icing sugar through a sieve to dust the waffles evenly.

OATIE BREAKFAST WAFFLES

Makes 8-10 waffles

INGREDIENTS

- 225g/8oz plain/all purpose flour
- 3 tbsp brown sugar
- 125g/4oz rolled oats
- 1 ½ tsp baking powder
- 1 tsp baking soda
- ½ tsp salt
- 370ml/1½ cups buttermilk
- 2 eggs, beaten
- 125g/4oz melted butter
- ½ tsp vanilla extract

METHOD

1 Add the flour, sugar, oats, baking powder, baking soda and salt to a large bowl & mix well

2 Add the buttermilk, eggs, vanilla extract and melted butter & stir well until you have a smooth batter. Add the melted butter and mix until combined.

3 Allow the batter to rest for at least 5 minutes and preheat your Waffle Maker.

4 When the waffle maker is fully heated pour approximately 90ml/⅓ cup of batter into the centre of each grid. Take care not to overfill the grids.

5 Close the lid and allow to cook for approx. 5 minutes or until the waffles are cooked through and piping hot

6 When the waffles are ready open the lid, carefully remove from the waffle maker and serve whilst still warm sprinkled with chopped walnuts.

CHEFS NOTE

These waffles make a great breakfast that will set you up for the day.

BASIC GLUTEN FREE WAFFLES

Makes 8-10 waffles

INGREDIENTS

- 400g/14oz gluten free plain/all purpose flour
- 1 tbsp baking powder
- 1 tsp baking soda
- ½ tsp salt
- 3 tbsp sugar
- 60ml/ ¼ cup vegetable oil
- 430ml/1 ¾ cup milk
- 2 eggs

METHOD

1 Add all the ingredients to a large bowl and mix well until you have a smooth batter.

2 Allow the batter to rest for at least 5 minutes and preheat your Waffle Maker.

3 When the waffle maker is fully heated pour approximately 90ml/⅓ cup of batter into the centre of each grid. Take care not to overfill the grids.

4 Close the lid and allow to cook for approx. 5 minutes or until the waffles are cooked through and piping hot

5 When the waffles are ready open the lid, carefully remove from the waffle maker and serve whilst still warm.

CHEFS NOTE

These simple waffles make a create gluten free base for your favourite toppings.

TRAIL MIX WAFFLES

Makes 8-10 waffles

INGREDIENTS

- 400g/14oz gluten free plain/all purpose flour
- 1 tbsp baking powder
- 1 tsp baking soda
- ½ tsp salt
- 3 tbsp sugar
- 60ml/¼ cup vegetable oil
- 430ml/1¾ cup milk
- 2 eggs
- 2 tbsp pumpkin seeds
- 1 tbsp chopped almonds
- 2 tbsp sunflower seeds
- 2 tbsp dried cranberries

METHOD

1 Add all the ingredients (except the seeds, nuts & cranberries) to a large bowl and mix well until you have a smooth batter.

2 Allow the batter to rest for at least 5 minutes and preheat your Waffle Maker.

3 Carefully fold through the pumpkins seeds, almond, sunflower seeds & cranberries until combined into the mixture.

4 When the waffle maker is fully heated pour approximately 90ml/⅓ cup of batter into the centre of each grid. Take care not to overfill the grids.

5 Close the lid and allow to cook for approx. 5 minutes or until the waffles are cooked through and piping hot

6 When the waffles are ready open the lid, carefully remove from the waffle maker and serve whilst still warm.

CHEFS NOTE

This trail mix waffle is gluten-free.

BLUEBERRY WHOLE WHEAT WAFFLES

Makes 8-10 waffles

INGREDIENTS

- 150g/5oz whole wheat flour
- 100g/3½oz plain/all purpose flour
- 2 tsp brown sugar
- 1 tbsp baking powder
- 1 tsp salt
- 2 eggs
- 340ml/1⅓ cups milk
- 75g/3oz melted butter
- 1 tsp vanilla extract
- 200g/7oz blueberries
- 1 tbsp icing sugar

METHOD

1 Add the whole wheat flour, plain flour, sugar, baking powder & salt to a large bowl and mix well.

2 In a separate bowl beat together the eggs, milk, melted butter and vanilla extract & stir this into the flour mixture until you have a smooth batter.

3 Gently fold through the blueberries until combined.

4 Allow the batter to rest for at least 5 minutes and preheat your Waffle Maker.

5 When the waffle maker is fully heated pour approximately 90ml/⅓ cup of batter into the centre of each grid. Take care not to overfill the grids.

6 Close the lid and allow to cook for approx. 5 minutes or until the waffles are cooked through and piping hot

7 When the waffles are ready open the lid, carefully remove from the waffle maker, dust with icing sugar and serve whilst still warm.

CHEFS NOTE

Blueberries hold well in waffles but try any soft berries you have to hand.

GRUYERE & POTATO SAVOURY WAFFLE

Makes 8-10 waffles

INGREDIENTS

- 250g/9oz plain/all purpose flour
- 1 tbsp sugar
- 1 tbsp baking powder
- 430ml/1¾ cups milk
- 100g/3½oz melted butter
- 3 eggs
- 200g/7oz cooked potatoes, roughly grated
- 75g/2oz Gruyere cheese, grated

METHOD

1 Add the flour, sugar & baking powder to a large bowl and mix well.

2 In a separate bowl beat together the milk, melted butter and eggs & stir this into the flour mixture until you have a smooth batter.

3 Gently fold the grated potatoes and cheese through the batter.

4 Allow the batter to rest for at least 5 minutes and preheat your Waffle Maker.

5 When the waffle maker is fully heated pour approximately 90ml/⅓ cup of batter into the centre of each grid. Take care not to overfill the grids.

6 Close the lid and allow to cook for approx. 5 minutes or until the waffles are cooked through and piping hot.

7 When the waffles are ready open the lid, carefully remove from the waffle maker and serve whilst still warm.

CHEFS NOTE

Make sure your cooked potatoes are cooled before adding to the batter.

69

PROTEIN PLUS SAVOURY WAFFLES

Makes 8-10 waffles

INGREDIENTS

- 250g/9oz plain/all purpose flour
- 2 scoops protein powder
- 1 tbsp sugar
- 1 tbsp baking powder
- 430ml/1¾ cups milk
- 100g/3½oz melted butter
- 3 eggs
- 2 tbsp chia seeds

METHOD

1 Add the flour, protein powder, sugar & baking powder to a large bowl and mix well.

2 In a separate bowl beat together the milk, melted butter and eggs & stir this into the flour mixture until you have a smooth batter.

3 Gently fold the chia seeds through the batter.

4 Allow the batter to rest for at least 5 minutes and preheat your Waffle Maker.

5 When the waffle maker is fully heated pour approximately 90ml/⅓ cup of batter into the centre of each grid. Take care not to overfill the grids.

6 Close the lid and allow to cook for approx. 5 minutes or until the waffles are cooked through and piping hot

7 When the waffles are ready open the lid, carefully remove from the waffle maker and serve whilst still warm.

CHEFS NOTE

A super post-gym waffle. Try with scrambled eggs for added protein .

CRANBERRY & PECAN OAT WAFFLES

Makes 8-10 waffles

INGREDIENTS

- 225g/8oz plain/all purpose flour
- 3 tbsp brown sugar
- 125g/4oz rolled oats
- 1½ tsp baking powder
- 1 tsp baking soda
- ½ tsp salt
- 370ml/1½ cups buttermilk
- 2 eggs, beaten
- 125g/4oz melted butter
- ½ tsp vanilla extract
- Handful dried cranberries
- Handful chopped pecans

METHOD

1 Add the flour, sugar, oats, baking powder, baking soda and salt to a large bowl & mix well.

2 Add the buttermilk, eggs, vanilla extract and melted butter & stir well until you have a smooth batter. Add the melted butter and mix until combined.

3 Allow the batter to rest for at least 5 minutes and preheat your Waffle Maker.

4 When the waffle maker is fully heated sprinkle a few of the cranberries and pecans onto the grids Pour approximately 90ml/⅓ cup of batter into the centre of each grid. Take care not to overfill the grids.

5 Close the lid and allow to cook for approx. 5 minutes or until the waffles are cooked through and piping hot

6 When the waffles are ready open the lid, carefully remove from the waffle maker and serve whilst still warm sprinkled with chopped walnuts.

CHEFS NOTE

A perfect pick-me-up waffle. Serve with yoghurt and a drizzle of honey.

FLAX SEED & BANANA WAFFLES

Makes 8-10 waffles

INGREDIENTS

- 300g/11oz plain/all purpose flour
- 2 tbsp caster sugar
- 2 tsp baking powder
- 1 tsp baking soda
- ½ tsp salt
- 2 eggs
- 90ml vegetable oil
- 200g/7oz crème fraiche
- 180ml/¾ cup buttermilk
- 2 ripe bananas
- 2 tsp flax seeds
- 1 tbsp icing sugar

METHOD

1 Add the flour, sugar, baking powder, baking soda & salt to a large bowl and mix well.

2 In a cup beat together the eggs and oil and add to the flour bowl along with the crème fraiche and buttermilk. Stir until you have a smooth batter.

3 Peel and mash the bananas with the back of a fork. Fold this into the batter along with the flax seeds until combined.

4 Allow the batter to rest for at least 5 minutes and preheat your Waffle Maker.

5 When the waffle maker is fully heated pour approximately 90ml/⅓ cup of batter into the centre of each grid. Take care not to overfill the grids.

6 Close the lid and allow to cook for approx. 5 minutes or until the waffles are cooked through and piping hot.

7 When the waffles are ready open the lid, carefully remove from the waffle maker. Dust with icing sugar and serve whilst still warm.

CHEFS NOTE

Flaxseeds, also called linseeds, are a rich source of omega-3.

CHRISTMAS SPICE WAFFLES

Makes 8-10 waffles

INGREDIENTS

- 300g/11oz plain/all purpose flour
- 1 tbsp brown sugar
- 2 tbsp baking powder
- ½ tsp baking soda
- 2 tsp ground cinnamon
- ¼ tsp ground cloves
- ½ tsp ground nutmeg
- ½ tsp salt
- 380ml/1½ cups skimmed milk
- 90ml/ ¾ cup vegetable oil
- 2 eggs, beaten
- 1 tbsp icing sugar

METHOD

1 Add all the ingredients, except the icing sugar, to a large bowl and mix well until you have a smooth batter.

2 Allow the batter to rest for at least 5 minutes and preheat your Waffle Maker.

3 When the waffle maker is fully heated pour approximately 90ml/⅓ cup of batter into the centre of each grid. Take care not to overfill the grids.

4 Close the lid and allow to cook for approx. 5 minutes or until the waffles are cooked through and piping hot

5 When the waffles are ready open the lid, carefully remove from the waffle maker, dust with icing sugar and serve whilst still warm.

CHEFS NOTE

Cinnamon, cloves and nutmeg are the holy trinity of Christmas spices.

PEPPERONI PIZZA WAFFLES

Makes 8-10 waffles

INGREDIENTS

- 250g/9oz plain/all purpose flour
- 1 tsp garlic powder
- 1 tbsp sugar
- 1 tbsp baking powder
- 430ml/1¾ cups milk
- 100g/3½oz melted butter
- 3 eggs
- 75g/3oz pepperoni, finely chopped
- 75g/3oz mozzarella shredded
- 2 tsp dried Italian herbs

METHOD

1 Add the flour, garlic powder, sugar & baking powder to a large bowl and mix well.

2 In a separate bowl beat together the milk, melted butter and eggs & stir this into the flour mixture until you have a smooth batter.

3 Gently fold the pepperoni, mozzarella and herbs through the batter.

4 Allow the batter to rest for at least 5 minutes and preheat your Waffle Maker.

5 When the waffle maker is fully heated pour approximately 90ml/⅓ cup of batter into the centre of each grid. Take care not to overfill the grids.

6 Close the lid and allow to cook for approx. 5 minutes or until the waffles are cooked through and piping hot

7 When the waffles are ready open the lid, carefully remove from the waffle maker and serve whilst still warm.

CHEFS NOTE

Try serving these pizza waffles with a spicy tomato dip.

74

HOMEMADE SYRUPS & FRUIT COMPOTES

ORANGE HONEY SYRUP

Makes 6 servings

INGREDIENTS

- 250ml/1 cup honey
- 1 orange
- Glass jar for storage

METHOD

1 Give the orange a rinse and carefully zest it.

2 Put the zest to one side and juice the orange.

3 Gently warm a saucepan on the hob and whisk the honey & orange juice together in the saucepan over a gentle heat.

4 Bring the syrup to the boil and keep on mixing until it's completely combined.

5 Take the pan off the heat and stir in the orange zest.

6 Leave the syrup to cool and thicken a little before serving.

CHEFS NOTE

It's best to use a free-flowing honey rather than a waxy honey for this syrup.

CHUNKY BLUEBERRY SYRUP

Makes 6 servings

INGREDIENTS

- 300g/11oz blueberries
- 120ml/½ cup water
- 150g/5oz sugar
- 1 tbsp lemon juice
- Glass jar for storage

METHOD

1 Remove the stems from the blueberries and give them a rinse.

2 Add the blueberries and water to a saucepan and simmer for 15 minutes on a gentle heat. Use a potato masher to bash and squeeze all the juice from the blueberries whilst they are in the pan.

3 Add the sugar to the pan and bring to the boil. Reduce the heat and leave to simmer for about 10 minutes or until the syrup thickens.

4 Add the lemon juice and cook for a minute longer.

5 Remove from the heat and leave the syrup to cool and thicken a little before serving.

CHEFS NOTE

If you want a smooth syrup without any chunky 'bits', pass the blueberry mixture through a sieve and discard the skins before adding the sugar.

CINNAMON SYRUP

Makes 6 servings

INGREDIENTS

- 175g/6oz brown sugar
- 120ml/½ cup water
- 50g/2oz butter
- 1 tsp ground cinnamon
- Glass jar for storage

METHOD

1 Gently warm a saucepan on the hob.

2 Whisk the sugar, water and cinnamon together in the saucepan over a gentle heat.

3 Slowly bring to the boil and keep on mixing until it's completely combined.

4 Take the pan off the heat and whisk in the butter.

5 Leave the syrup to cool and thicken a little before serving or storing in a glass jar.

CHEFS NOTE

Cinnamon syrup makes a lovely topping over waffles with sliced bananas.

VANILLA SYRUP

Makes 6 servings

INGREDIENTS

- 175g/6oz brown sugar
- 120ml/½ cup water
- ½ tsp vanilla extract
- 50g/2oz butter
- Glass jar for storage

METHOD

1 Gently warm a saucepan on the hob.

2 Whisk the sugar, water and vanilla together in the saucepan over a gentle heat.

3 Slowly bring to the boil and keep on mixing until it's completely combined.

4 Take the pan off the heat and whisk in the butter.

5 Leave the syrup to cool and thicken a little before serving.

CHEFS NOTE

Vanilla syrup is a classic sweet waffle topping. Pair it up with vanilla ice cream too.

NO COOK SUGAR FREE SYRUP

Makes 6 servings

INGREDIENTS

- 250ml/1 cup water
- 2 tsp maple essence
- 2 tsp lemon juice
- ½ tsp stevia extract
- 1/3 tsp Xanthan gum
- Pinch of salt
- Glass jar for storage

METHOD

1 Place the water, maple flavor and stevia into a blender and blend for a few seconds.

2 Drop the Xanthan gum and salt in and blend for a few seconds more until everything is combined.

3 This needs leaving for a while now so pour into a jar and place in the fridge overnight. In the morning it will be ready to use.

CHEFS NOTE

Xantham gum is a food thickener popular in gluten free diets. It is now widely available in health food stores.

GLUTEN FREE SALTED CARAMEL SYRUP

INGREDIENTS

- 200g/7oz brown sugar
- 60ml/¼ cup water
- 50g/2oz unsalted butter
- 120ml/½ cup double cream
- 1 ½ tsp sea salt
- Glass jar for storage

METHOD

1 Gently warm a saucepan on the hob.

2 Whisk the sugar and honey together in the saucepan over a medium heat.

3 Bring the syrup to the boil and keep on whisking until it becomes a rich golden brown colour.

4 Take the pan off the heat and whisk in the butter, followed by the cream and salt.

5 Leave to cool and thicken a little before serving.

CHEFS NOTE

Pair this with the basic gluten free waffle recipe on page 66 and serve with berries.

PEACH & CINNAMON COMPOTE

Makes 6 servings

INGREDIENTS

- 300g/11oz tinned peaches
- 120ml/½ cup fresh orange juice
- 2 tbsp brown sugar
- ½ tsp ground cinnamon
- 75g/3oz strawberries
- Glass jar for storage

METHOD

1 Drain the peaches and cut into bite-sized chunks.

2 Add the peaches, orange juice, sugar and cinnamon to a saucepan and bring to the boil.

3 Reduce the heat, add the strawberries and simmer for 10-15 minutes on a gentle heat until the compote thickens.

4 Remove from the heat and leave the syrup to cool and thicken a little more before serving.

CHEFS NOTE

Use whichever berries you have to hand to add to the peaches.

FESTIVE DRIED FRUIT COMPOTE

INGREDIENTS

- 450g/1lb dried mixed fruit
- 250ml/1 cup boiling water
- 60m/¼ cup fresh orange juice
- 3 tbsp brown sugar
- ½ tsp ground cinnamon
- ¼ tsp vanilla essence
- Pinch of ground cloves
- Glass jar for storage

METHOD

1 Add the dried fruit to a bowl along with the boiling water and leave to soak for an hour or two.

2 After this time drain the fruit and place in a saucepan along with all the other ingredients.

3 Add 60ml/¼ cup of water and bring to the boil.

4 Reduce the heat and gently simmer for 40-50 minutes until the compote thickens.

5 Remove from the heat and leave to cool a little before serving.

CHEFS NOTE

Try adding a large splash of cognac if you wish before bringing the fruit to the boil.

MAPLE BERRY COMPOTE

INGREDIENTS

- 300g/11oz mixed berries
- 60ml/¼ cup maple syrup
- 1 tsp vanilla essence
- 2 tbsp lemon juice
- Glass jar for storage

METHOD

1 Add all the ingredients to a saucepan and bring to the boil (add a splash of water if you feel it needs it).

2 Reduce the heat and simmer for 10-15 minutes on a gentle heat until the berries begin to loose their shape

3 Remove from the heat and leave the to cool and thicken a little more before serving.

CHEFS NOTE

A mix of strawberries and blueberries work well for this compote. Adjust the maple syrup to suit your own taste.

RHUBARB COMPOTE

Makes 6 servings

INGREDIENTS

- 300g/11oz rhubarb
- 75g/3oz strawberries
- 60ml/¼ cup water
- 150g/5oz sugar
- Glass jar for storage

METHOD

1 Chop the rhubarb into bite-size chunks, hull and halve the strawberries.

2 Add the rhubarb, water and sugar to a saucepan and simmer for 15 minutes on a gentle heat.

3 Add the strawberries, cover and simmer for a further 10-15 minutes or until the rhubarb is tender.

4 Remove from the heat and to cool and thicken a little before serving.

CHEFS NOTE

Rhubarb can be quite sharp so make sure the compote is sweet enough by adjusting the sugar quantity.

OTHER COOKNATION TITLES

If you enjoyed I Love My Waffle Maker *you may also like other titles in the* I♥MY *series.*

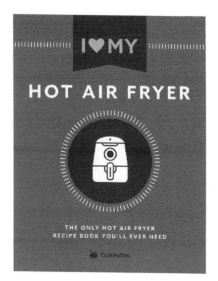

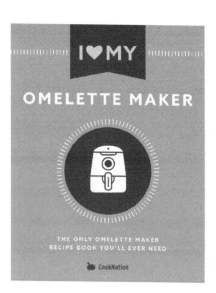

To browse the full catalogue visit
www.bellmackenzie.com

Printed in Great Britain
by Amazon